Inspired BY Love
Living Life with Faith

Anne Goodsell Love

Anne Love

InspiringVoices®
A Service of **Guideposts**

Inspiring Voices books may be ordered through booksellers or by contacting:

Inspiring Voices
1663 Liberty Drive
Bloomington, IN 47403
www.inspiringvoices.com
1-(866) 697-5313

All images are by Mark Berkley, used with permission.

ISBN: 978-1-4624-0163-5 (sc)
ISBN: 978-1-4624-0162-8 (e)

Library of Congress Control Number: 2012939310

Printed in the United States of America

Inspiring Voices rev. date: 06/05/2012

Contents

Acknowledgements

Many people have encouraged me along the way to publishing this book; I thank them from the bottom of my heart. My sons, Conor and Garrett, are a source of joy and inspiration. My parents, Millard and Irene Goodsell, have been cheerleaders for me all my life; thanks Mom and Dad! Friends Leslie Kantor and Carol Van Der Karr were the first to encourage me to start a blog. Susan Watson helped me to create the title of the blog. Jeremiah Tanious, my writing buddy, has "been a stand for me" to follow my desire to write. John Van Der Karr is a constant source of joy and love.

Inspiration and ideas come from my participation in the life of Prospect Presbyterian Church, which is led with tremendous talent and love by Rick Boyer, Rita Boyer, Jason Asbury, and a large cast of other "church family" members. Other friends are a source of strength and laughter—thanks to Chris DeMarco, Caroline Farnsworth, Rick Noll, Candace Snyder, David Snyder, Stacy Mevs, and Robin M. Similarly, many co-workers have been instrumental in giving me confidence and sharing their lives with me - Ruta Shah-Gordon, Maddy Sliger, Dina Assante, Candy Pucci, Camille Cook, Ann Giarratano, Dorine Trivelli, Margaret Echanique, Natalie Johnson, Victoria Crispo, Tulin Aldas, Mary Zanfini, Cass Freedland, Curtis Wright, Sabrina Slater, Sara Klein, Letty Romero, Richard Guarasci, Devorah Lieberman, Sofia Pertuz, and Catharine McGlade – thanks and love to you all. Thanks to Mark Berkley for following his desire to capture the beauty of nature with his photography, and for sharing his work in this book.

And thanks be to God from whom all blessings flow.

Introduction

"Welcome to Inspiring Voices!" said Caleb, the publishing consultant. "We'll get you all set up and give you access to the Writer's Resource Room, which includes over 500 articles and resource items so that you can fully step into the world of being an author. It's a great collection of material and I'm sure you're really going to be excited to see what's in there!" Clearly, he is excited about offering me this resource, and he thinks I'm going to love it. What I'm thinking is, *Holy cow! I have to read 500 things in the process of writing this book?! This is going to be a lot more complicated than I thought.*

So began the publication process for this book. The writing process started a few years ago, with a desire to write about the small joys and wonders of life. I am a college administrator and the mother of two teenage boys. I had been reading inspirational essays and daily devotionals for many years, but I started to hear myself composing my own essays in my head as I was gardening, walking my dog, or driving to work. I wrote "Sunrise Reflection" and sent it to a few family members and friends who liked it and encouraged me to write more. After writing a few more, friends suggested that I start a blog and gradually I added to it. A fellow coach in a Landmark Education course, who was starting a writing project of his own, proposed that we have weekly check-in phone calls to hold each other accountable for the goals we were setting, and that combination of structure and encouragement prompted me to keep on writing.

I get ongoing encouragement from my church family at Prospect Presbyterian Church, and from family, friends, and co-workers. I also get encouragement from the writing process itself, and from the close connection I feel to God when I truly let down my guard and allow myself to feel God's presence. Exploring my feelings—joy and sadness, courage and fear, laughter and tears—has sharpened my sense of connection to other people and to God. Having grown up in Connecticut, born to and raised by loving Yankee Protestants who live by the motto of "less talk, more action," I never thought I would profess my faith outside of the walls of my church, but the fiery furnace of a divorce made me realize that I need to follow my dreams, and be bold and powerful in the process.

I invite you to explore your own life as you read these reflections, and I encourage you to capture your thoughts, hopes, and dreams in writing before they swirl away in the face of fear, uncertainty, or doubt. Be courageous in declaring actions you will take, connections you will make or renew, new directions you will explore. We have one life to live, and while I am all for careful planning, preparation, and decision making, at some point—if we want to live a life of fulfillment and purpose—we have to take responsibility for our own future and take steps toward it. We won't move forward every day, and sometimes we'll take steps back or to the side, but I believe that over time, a slow and steady forward march wins the race.

Being persistent, having faith, clinging to hope, facing our fears—these are the ways to keep moving forward. As a person of faith, I have the assurance that I am not alone in my journey, and the confidence to say that neither are you. I pray that you will find inspiration and motivation in these pages. Dream big, act boldly, reach out to others, and rejoice often!

Being Loving

Extravagance

"Everyone serves the good wine first, and then the inferior wine after the guests have become drunk. But you have kept the good wine until now" (John 2:10).

Recently my kids and I had drinks at a bookstore café. I looked at the prices on the menu and realized that blended drinks were $0.40 more than regular drinks. So I ordered the regular chai tea latte with milk and cinnamon. Then when the barista asked me if I wanted cinnamon syrup ($0.50) or cinnamon powder (no extra charge), I chose the powder. My son sipped his drink and asked me if I had ordered what he had asked for, as it tasted different. I said yes and suggested that he could add more sugar (no extra charge) if needed. He did so, but still it didn't taste like what he wanted. We read our books, drank our drinks, and had a nice enough time, but he drank about half his drink and then gave up.

I thought about this episode the next day as I read in Scripture about the miracle that Jesus performed at the wedding in Cana. When the wine ran out during the reception, Jesus' mother urged him to do something about it. He made wine out of water—and not only that, but he also made really good wine! This story appears early in the book of John and is listed as the first of Jesus' signs, or miracles. From the start, he does things in a big way—not necessarily a big, flashy way, but with a big heart. The actions of Jesus demonstrate God's extravagant love for all people.

I thought about how and where I demonstrate God's extravagant love. I felt pretty good about paying $3.10 for one drink until I remembered that my son hadn't really liked it.

I had wanted us to have an enjoyable afternoon, and we had, but my stinginess had prevented him from having a really enjoyable time. And I had saved $0.50 or $0.90? Fortunately, that amount does not make or break our budget for the month, but I had behaved as if it would. I know that there are many appropriate times to watch my pennies and dollars, but in hindsight, that was not one of them. Later, I apologized to him for my stinginess and he appreciated my candor. But I got a good reminder that money spent for an inferior product (not what my son really wanted) is money wasted. More importantly, gifts given with half a heart do not reflect the extravagance that I receive from God. I am blessed with much, and I believe that I am called to give much. Especially at this time, when scarcity is the experience of many people in our world, and fear of scarcity is in the hearts and minds of others, I need to live and give with a whole heart.

Lord, when I am tempted to be stingy, remind me of your extravagant love. Help me to live and give with an extravagant spirit. Amen.

E-cards and Greetings Cards

"AND NOW FAITH, HOPE, and love abide, these three; and the greatest of these is love" (1 Corinthians 13:13).

I haven't been a big fan of e-cards. I think it might have something to do with the ease with which they can be sent. This tells you something about my family's Puritan roots and our adherence to a strong work ethic. (Translation: if it takes hard work, it has value.) My aversion to e-cards also may be related to the fact that they come into my e-mail inbox which I often feel is overflowing already. *One more e-mail*, I sometimes think, *is not what I need!*

Today, however, as I started to think about sending Valentine's Day cards, I thought of how greeting cards might have seemed when they were created. Prior to greeting cards, people sent letters or notes, and they had to come up with the words all by themselves. Greeting cards added pictures, and that probably was a welcome addition. They also added words. What a revolutionary idea! All you had to do was add your name! But I'll bet that not everyone thought greeting cards were such a hot idea—so impersonal, you know? Someone else wrote the words. All you had to do was buy one, sign it, and send it.

And so it goes. New ideas gain traction—slowly at first. Maybe greeting cards were for birthdays first, then cards were added for sympathy, thank-yous, anniversaries, and weddings. Now you can buy a greeting card for almost any occasion or day of the week. And now I can see how an e-card is no less a message of love than a greeting card that arrives in the mailbox at my house. It has been selected just for me and sent because someone was thinking of me and wanted me to know. Not only that, but e-cards are free! My ancestors would be proud.

Lord, thank you for prayer, which is the epitome of fast, free, loving communication. Amen.

Comfort

COMFORT: "TO GIVE STRENGTH and hope to; to ease the grief or trouble of; a feeling of relief or encouragement" (www. merriam-webster.com).

I was exhausted. The first week of June had been very difficult. A close friend at work left for another job, my car broke down and was beyond repair, and my beloved dog Lacey died. I cried a little about my friend leaving, I cried buckets of tears over Lacey dying, and those events put the car situation into perspective, so I just went ahead and bought a new (used) car with very little drama.

In and around the events of that week were days and moments of uplifting grace, hope, and joy. The prior two weekends were filled with travel to see friends and family, some who I had not seen for years. I went to a friend's wedding and visited with cousins. My parents visited my home, and I went to my twenty-fifth college reunion. It was wonderful to reconnect with so many loved ones. It was a gift to travel to places of my younger days and revel in the shared experiences and memories.

Those high moments of reconnection gave me a reservoir of energy and strength for the low moments of loss and grief. Not to be overlooked were other gestures of grace and kindness woven throughout that week of trial. When my car broke down my former husband loaned me his car for a few days, as he could commute to work by train. My co-workers wrote sympathy cards and printed and framed a wonderful poem, "If a dog were your teacher," which now hangs on my kitchen wall. I celebrated another co-worker's birthday, and I talked with friends.

When I felt at my lowest, I was not alone. Friends and family, both near and far, were ready to lend an ear, shoulder, or hand. And as Rick Boyer, the minister of my church, reminds the congregation at the end of every worship service, God is always near us. He says, "God is at work in our lives—in all the moments and circumstances of our lives. The question is whether we are open to the movement of God's spirit among us, within us, and through us." Through the words and deeds of friends and family I can rest in God's comfort, be relieved of grief, and be refreshed by love, hope, and encouragement.

The poem "If a dog were your teacher" ends with these words: "When someone is having a bad day, be silent, sit closely, and nuzzle them gently." I say, amen.

Being Like Luna

"IF YOU SEE SOMEONE without a smile, give them one of yours" (Unknown).

Recently I attended a show at the theater on the campus where I work. During intermission, I saw a co-worker standing in the aisle, so I waved and called out, "Hello, Jim!" The man standing in front of him must have been named Jim too, because he gave me a big friendly wave and his smile lit up his face. What was I to do—Ignore him? Tell him that I wasn't really saying hello to him? Or walk up to him, say hello again, and introduce myself? I did the third option, giving him an equally big smile and asking him if he was enjoying the show. I gave a big hello to the woman by his side, who looked a little puzzled but was very polite. Then I went on and said hello to my co-worker, and chuckled to myself about the mix-up.

While telling my sons about the incident after the show, I described the man as "kind of like Luna," our new dog. She'll wag her tail for anybody and sidle up for some petting if the person is willing. It doesn't matter that she hasn't met the person before. She's not worried that the person won't recognize her or doesn't know her name. Luna is friendly without conditions. And the man was like that—unconcerned that he had never met me before, only responding to my friendly overture. What a great way to greet everyone we encounter! What a great way to start every day, every week, and every month—with no fear of rebuttal or rebuff but with a heartfelt hello to all.

Now, truth be told, I am like Luna a lot of the time—friendly, optimistic, happy. Luna, in her one-year-old, not-yet-a-grown-up-dog way, welcomes people with abandon. I have more reserve—the caution built up over time and from experience. I know that not everyone responds like Luna or the very friendly gentleman at the theater. But Luna's puppy-like attitude is infectious, and I'll seek to emulate it in the coming days. Winter is coming just around the corner, so enthusiastically extending my hands in friendship to others will be a good way to keep my hands, and theirs, warm.

Lord, thank you for the gift of friendship. At this time of year, it is good to be reminded that this gift is free, without an expiration date, and infectious in a good way. Amen.

Civility

"Do to others as you would have them do to you" (Luke 6:31).

Three cars drove by me after I slowed and stopped my car as the traffic light changed from yellow to red. They were behind me, they drove around my car and other cars that had stopped for the light, and drove right on through. No emergency lights or sirens to explain this behavior. I got really mad, as this happens with some frequency in that particular area, and if I had some sort of remote control device that would blow out their tires I would have used it with great satisfaction. What really burned me up about these cars driving through the red light was their reckless disregard for others—disregard for the safety of others, and disregard for those of us waiting our turn to go. Their behavior seemed to indicate that they thought the rules of the road didn't apply to them. They behaved as if they were more important than the rest of us who were stopped at the light. I stewed about this as I drove on and parked my car, and I realized that this is one way that incivility begins.

I should interject here that at work there had been some racially-charged incidents that were shocking and upsetting. The incidents had gotten many of us to be thinking about the environment at work that would allow for smaller incidents to go unchecked and unreported until they grew to be a direct threat to a member of our community. Discussion groups were held, which resulted in fruitful dialogues that uncovered more accounts of people being slighted, ignored, pushed aside, or silenced. We are continuing to work to uncover assumptions and biases—the underlying thoughts that can emerge as thoughtless and hurtful actions and words—but it will require courage, trust, and time to build and rebuild relationships so that we can establish a healthier and more respectful environment.

It was against this backdrop that I tried to turn my thoughts of vengeance (blowing out the tires of those three cars) to thoughts of insight and understanding. If being passed while sitting at a red light had gotten me that mad, how mad would people get at being treated disrespectfully or unfairly for days and months and years at a time? How many times does someone swallow a hurt or a humiliation before it erupts out of them in rage? Eventually we may take matters into our own hands and lash out in hurt and anger against others who have wronged us.

Jesus' teaching on how we should treat our enemies is clear: love them. It is easy to love those who we love, but the Golden Rule is about treating everyone well, not just those we like, or those we hope to impress. It is not up to us to pick and choose who gets favored treatment and who does not. But I think that in order to live by the Golden Rule and all that it implies, I have to believe truly that God is in charge. I have to have faith that God cares about me and will watch over me, and that God's justice will prevail in the world. Notice that I said God's justice, not my justice, or the justice that my friends and I think is appropriate. Having faith in God's justice requires that I acknowledge that I don't know what's best for everyone (and of course, I do think this way much of the time).

So why did I get so mad when three cars passed me at the red light? They behaved as if they were more important than me, that's why. And why would I care about feeling important?

What if I was feeling unimportant that day? What if I was feeling powerless in the face of the incidents at work that were filled with anger and hatred? Then it makes sense that another incident that emphasized my perception of being unimportant or powerless would set me off down the path of vengeance and violence.

If, however, I truly believe that I am important in God's eyes, and that I have power in my life, then I can alter my perceptions of others. I can see them not as threats to me but as fellow travelers who are experiencing their own doubts, uncertainties, and pain, and then I can respond with tolerance, forbearance, kindness, and love.

God, I know that I am important in your eyes, but often I forget. Help me to live out the Golden Rule every day, that by doing so others will know how important they are to you too. Amen.

Making The Bed

"Like good stewards of the manifold grace of God, serve one another with whatever gift each of you has received" (1 Peter 4:10).

One day a number of years ago I made my son's bed. Really, I re-made it, straightening the sheets, pulling up the covers, digging a stuffed animal out from between the mattress and the wall and placing it on the pillow. I didn't usually make his bed and neither did he and we both lived our days quite happily, but it just struck me as a nice thing to do at that moment. I like to make my bed. It gives me a sense of order and organization that relaxes me.

After making his bed I got an inkling of the joy to be had in doing a small gesture of kindness for another person. As a divorced mom I see my kids for half of the week, and as a working mom the time we have together on week days is short. I don't spend much time with housekeeping chores. But at that moment I understood the satisfaction to be had in that activity. I wasn't making the bed because it was messy, I was doing it because I wanted to give him a feeling of relaxation when he walked into his room. Maybe he'd feel relaxed, maybe he wouldn't, or maybe he wouldn't even realize that the bed had been made, but I saw it as a way to express love.

I had not thought before that being a mom means that I minister to my children as I attend to their wants and needs. Of course, I knew that I take care of them, but I hadn't used the word "minister" in that context before. As a Protestant Christian I usually think of ministering as something done by the minister of the church, or by the deacons, or by church members through a church activity, but I understood in that moment that to provide a service to others is to provide ministry, and that's what makes it satisfying. When I keep in mind that I am living out my Christian values and expressing my love in the acts of service that I carry out, then I get the joy of ministry. I serve God by serving others in all the different ways that are available to me every day.

Lord, let me be of service to you today. Amen.

Being Courageous

Luna

"Jesus, looking at him, loved him and said, 'You lack one thing; go, sell what you own, and give the money to the poor, and you will have treasure in heaven; then come, follow me'" (Mark 10:21).

My kids and I got a dog. We had been thinking about getting another dog for a while, but with summer travels and then the start of school the timing wasn't right. Frankly, I was a little worried about the added responsibility of a pet. It was nice to be pet-free for a while, not worrying about running home after work to let the dog outside, and not having to pooper-scoop the back yard. But it was lonely when the boys were away, and when I mentioned that it might be time to get another dog they were really excited. So we went to the animal shelter and she picked us out, really. She came out of her cage, wagged her tail as she walked toward us, and flopped down for a belly rub. We named her Luna, and she has been a friendly, energetic addition to our family. I met more people in the first week while walking with her in my neighborhood than I had met in the past 5 months!

While I was still in the stage of thinking about getting another dog, it occurred to me that the process of getting a dog was somewhat like my experience of letting Jesus into my life. I would do it if it was not too disruptive, but if it was going to take a lot of time, energy, and aggravation, then maybe I wasn't up for it. Maybe I would keep *thinking* about doing it, and *say* that I would do it later. Meanwhile, I was denying myself and my kids the joy of letting a dog into our lives and hearts.

Similarly, I can say I'll let Jesus into my life and heart, but in truth I'm not sure I'm up for it if it will be too risky. I do have my moments of acceptance—those times I raise my hand and volunteer for something out of my comfort zone—but I have more moments of complacency, where I live my life in the status quo, enjoying what I have and not looking for change. Most days I am like the wealthy man who walked away from Jesus upon finding out that to enter the kingdom of heaven he would have to sell all he had. I like what I have! If following Jesus is too radical of a change, I'm going to think about it for a long time before I act.

But as I reflect on the process of getting a dog and how I could have thought about it for months and even years, I wonder what I am missing out on when I think too long about letting Jesus into my heart. By holding Jesus at a distance, letting him in when it is comfortable, or predictable, or convenient, what joys am I denying myself? What am I denying others? Where are you holding back in your life, afraid to put that next step forward for yourself and others because of what it might take?

Lord, sometimes I think too much. Let me also pay attention to the urgings of my heart. Amen.

Telling My Story

"In the beginning was the Word, and the Word was with God, and the Word was God" (John 1:1).

I love words. I love to read them, I love to write them. How powerful they can be! Words can inspire, help, guide, and create. They also can hurt, harm, and destroy. Words unspoken can cause a person to feel regret, while words spoken can cause a person to feel relief, excitement, joy. As God created all things with the Word, we create our feelings with our words.

In a shop I saw a tile with the phrase "The world is waiting to hear your story." I felt a thrill of anticipation and eagerness tinged with doubt. *Really?* I thought, *the world is waiting to hear my story?* I didn't buy the tile, partly because I was Christmas shopping and I was focusing on gifts for others, but also partly because I was scared—scared to look at that statement every day and feel pressure to write my story!

Maybe the tinge of fear I felt was a little bit like what Moses felt like when he was in the presence of God. *Really?* Moses might have thought, *God is allowing me to be in his presence? Really*, I say back to my doubting self, *I am in God's presence every moment of every day*. I believe that we all are, whether we choose to believe it or not. And it's not so much that the world is *waiting* to hear my story—the world spins around whether I write or speak or not—but the world would very much *like* to hear my story, because it's one of a gazillion stories of God's work on earth. These stories are filled with all the stuff of best-selling novels—love overcoming hate; hope overcoming fear; lovers, friends, and families reconnecting after distance or judgment has kept them apart.

So today I will endeavor to live my day with the knowledge that God is my co-author. I will live today's part of my story and not worry so much about how it will be reviewed by others. (*Will the critics acclaim it as a best-seller or not?*) For one thing, it's the only story I've got and no one else's to tell. For another thing, with God as my co-author, I can be completely confident that I am equipped to live a life worth telling.

Lord, thanks for a new day and a clean page upon which to live and write our story. Amen.

Show Up

"You are the light of the world... No one after lighting a lamp puts it under the bushel basket, but on the lampstand, and it gives light to all in the house. In the same way, let your light shine before others..." (Matthew 5:14-16).

My son joined a high school team, and I am very proud of him for that. Not proud because it is a sport, but because he didn't know anyone on the team and he went anyway. He was nervous, but his dad and I encouraged him, and after the first day he was comfortable. This says a lot for the team and its organizers who set a welcoming tone. My son has told me of other students who also showed up and are playing, and others who showed up and played for a while and then left to join another group or team that was better suited to them.

I applaud them all. They are learning an important life lesson—that showing up truly is a very big part of what it takes to be successful in life. And I don't mean what it takes to earn a lot of money, although that may happen too. When we join an organization or a team, a church or a musical group, we are extending ourselves and joining a community, and we need all the community we can get! When we go to a class, we are affirming our place in that group; when we attend a second and third meeting of an organization and sign up to help with an event, we are not just letting that group make a claim on our time and energy, but we are saying that we matter. We want to be recognized by others around us, but sometimes we fear that we won't be seen or included, so we don't even show up. Sometimes we'd rather choose to be alone than show up and not be included. Our fear of rejection—of failing to make that connection—is huge.

Showing up at a meeting of a group takes some courage, even if you've gotten an invitation. But just as much as you're thinking that you need them—you really want to be on that team, or you really want to be a part of the planning committee for your town's celebration—they need you! Healthy organizations need new members, new ideas, and new infusions of energy to thrive. They may not know it when you first walk through the door, or step onto the field, but you may be the very thing that's needed. And if you're not, there's another group out there waiting for your contributions of ideas, energy, friendship, and other gifts and talents. Be courageous today and show up to somewhere that you've been wanting to go. Maybe it's to a family member's home, but you've been afraid to go there. Maybe it's to a class or a group that you were attending but got away from and now you're afraid to go back. Show up! No one else can do it for you, and your presence really will matter.

Lord, give me courage to show up and be counted. Amen.

Being Patient

Amarylis Or Oak Tree?

"FOR EVERYTHING THERE IS a season, and a time for every purpose under heaven ... a time to plant, and a time to pluck up what is planted" (Ecclesiastes 3:1-2).

Starting new romantic relationships can be challenging. Once you find someone (a challenge in and of itself!) the process and pace of getting to know that person is a process that unfolds as you both reach out, respond, and react to each other.

While reading a devotional by Marilyn Morgan King about the Scripture above, I got a great image of how a new relationship is like a new plant. It starts out as a seed, needing some time for a root to grow, a shoot to sprout. Then it becomes a tender seedling, needing some warmth from the sun, some rain, and time to get adjusted to its environment. Too much heat too soon can result in a withered seedling, just as too much rain can result in moldy roots – neither condition being right for the seedling to grow into a healthy plant.

Of course, different plants require different growing conditions. A past relationship of mine was like an amaryllis. It took off fast, thrived with lots of food and drink, emerged into a showy, bright flower, but ultimately was unsustainable. The hothouse conditions of that relationship produced short-term excitement. While it lasted, both of us had a great time, but it didn't have the conditions needed for it to thrive for the long run.

Perhaps an oak tree is a better plant to emulate in a relationship. It takes time for the acorn, dropped onto the cold winter ground, to soften with the spring's moisture and warmth. It takes time to put down a root and for a shoot to emerge, foretelling the development of a tree trunk. It needs sunlight to grow, but its true nature will not emerge in its first season, or even its second. It will take time to grow and develop, always changing shape and size but always an oak, a mighty tree that can withstand wind, rain, drought, and heat.

Lord, in starting a new relationship I will resolve to be patient, giving the process time, and remembering that my aim is to nurture something more like an oak than an amaryllis. Amen.

2,200 Acorns

"Trust in the Lord, and do good; … take delight in the Lord, and he will give you the desires of your heart … Be still before the Lord, and wait patiently for him" (Psalm 37:3-4, and 7).

I have resolved to be patient in starting a new romantic relationship, and to imagine it like the growth of an oak tree—slow at first, but steady, developing into a strong plant whose roots run deep. A plant that, over time, will grow sturdy enough to withstand the buffeting winds of the weather, and can change and grow with the seasons but always is an oak tree.

This was a helpful image as I started dating, and by the fourth date with one man I was looking forward confidently to more dates and greater intimacy. Until he told me that he had started dating someone else and wouldn't be going on date number five with me! That's when I thought about oak trees and all the acorns they produce. A mature oak can produce an average of 2,200 acorns each year. This doesn't mean that all 2,200 of those acorns will become trees. Some will fall in water and rot, some will fall onto rocks and won't get enough nutrients, and many will get eaten by animals. Even those that make it to the dirt won't all become trees because there's not enough fertile soil where they are dropped, and not enough room. So not every acorn that is created becomes a tree, and that's okay. Nature's balance does not require that every acorn becomes a tree.

Mapping this acorn example onto dating relationships, however, can be depressing! Do I have to nurture 2,200 dating relationships to find one that will last? Other metaphors that come to mind are no more helpful. "You've got to kiss a lot of frogs before you find your handsome prince" (yuck). "There are more fish in the sea" (a lot more than 2,200!). Not helpful.

So how to sort through all the acorns to find one that has a really good chance of becoming a tree? How to find a man to date with whom I have a good chance of building a relationship that will last? Of course, many men and I are not a match because of geography, age difference, and such. But even with the aid of an internet site that can do that kind of screening, there are a lot of potential dates in my local area (352 in a recent search on just one internet dating site).

I suppose if I knew the answer then I wouldn't be writing this essay. But although I don't know the definitive answer, I have thought of some principles related to it:

- I can't tell just by looking. Yes, I can be attracted to someone by looking at him, but I can't know his inner nature from his outer appearance.

- It takes time. Sure, there are stories of love at first sight, but even those relationships take time to develop and mature. People usually are on their best behavior during the first dates, so it may take a while for the not-so-brilliant facets of our personalities to emerge.

- Timing is important. Acorns don't start growing in the winter, and perhaps if I am experiencing an emotional period like winter then that won't be a great time to cultivate a new relationship. I can have confidence, however, that spring always comes—always. There will be a prime time for an intimate relationship to grow.

- Being too serious doesn't help. Taking the acorn idea somewhat literally, I can remind myself to be a little nutty in this search for a spirited and solid relationship. Have fun with it and remember to laugh often.

- Ask for help. The first step to finding a man was meeting some men, and I wasn't doing much of that on my own. I needed some nudging to put a profile on an internet dating site, and my friends were encouraging and supportive. I asked friends and family to be on the lookout for possible dates.

- Trust God. For me this is the hardest, as it forces me to acknowledge that I don't have all the control, or even the majority of the control. I can be open to meeting new people, and active in meeting new people, and after that I have a choice. I can choose to be content with how the process unfolds, or I can choose to be anxious and impatient. I can live in faith that God will give me the desires of my heart (especially if I am sharing my desires with God faithfully in prayer), or I can pretend that I'm on my own. Trusting God is another version of asking for help, and believing that God will respond.

To bring it back to the metaphor of the acorns, I can be daunted by the prospect of sorting through all 2,200 of them, or I can be assured that in time, at the right time, an oak tree will grow. God's plan will unfold.

Lord, with your assurance, I will choose to be confident and relaxed, enjoying the wonderful people who are in my life already. Amen.

Stop Lights

"FOR A THOUSAND YEARS in your sight are like yesterday when it is past, or like a watch in the night" (Psalm 90:4).

While we were driving on the streets of my town the other day, my son remarked "You know, Mom, you never get stopped at a red light." Then he laughed and said, "That's because you don't drive on streets with traffic lights!" He's right, in that I've developed the habit of driving on side streets, making a few more turns and sometimes stopping at a few stop signs, but avoiding the lights. Like delivery drivers who are trained to make right turns only and thereby not wait to cross traffic to make a left turn, I've trained myself to take roads with fewer obstacles.

How does this apply to my life beyond driving a car? One answer is, if I'm getting stopped frequently on the "road" I'm on, I can take another route. It might seem like a longer route, but it might be smoother, or faster, or have a better view. It might take me past places I've not known about, but now can enrich my life.

Another answer involves how I view the time that I have to spend stopped at a traffic light, since I can't always avoid them. Sometimes I spend my time in aggravation, saying things like "How long is this going to take?" "Come on, let's go!" and "This is ridiculous!" Sometimes I look with a critical eye at the cars, people, and buildings around me, letting my aggravation and impatience cloud my view with a film of criticism. But sometimes I am at peace with the stops, taking a moment to pause, breathe deeply, pray, and view the people and things around me with curiosity and appreciation. I'm still stopped, but my attitude is completely different.

Of course, being stopped in life is different than being stopped at a traffic light. Even when the light seems to be taking forever to change, we know it will change in a few minutes. Our stops in life are not so predictable, and while we can be assured that the only constant in our lives is change, we aren't always privy to the schedule. We ask questions without sure answers: "When will I start feeling better?" "When will I find another job?" or "When will this [insert your pain here] be over?"

But although our stops in life have some differences compared to traffic light stops, the similarities are there too. When stopped in life, we can try another route, being open to side streets that seem less direct. We can wait with an attitude of appreciation and curiosity for where we're stopped. And we can remember to pray, even when it seems that no answers are forthcoming. Change is constant and ever present, and so is God.

Creator God, it seems that impatience is a theme in my life. Help me to use the times when I'm stopped to draw close to you. Amen.

Asking For Help

The Parental Juggling Act

"Ask, and it will be given to you; search, and you will find; knock, and the door will be opened for you" (Matthew 7:7).

Yesterday morning's phone call was brief and to the point. "Hi, Anne? When you are picking up my older son to go to the Music Marathon, can you pick up my younger son too and have him hang out with you for the afternoon until our other friends pick him up to take him to the school play? I've got to be at work."

I said sure, since I already was dropping off my older son, picking up my younger son, and well, you get the picture. Paint my car bright yellow and call it a school bus—that was yesterday's theme. I was happy that my main plan for the day was to go to the Music Marathon to hear my kids play their instruments with the orchestra and band, and that I was available to help out my friend and his kids. All of us had a lot to do, and with everyone's coordination and willingness, everyone got where they needed to go and no one got lost or forgotten!

When reflecting on my busy day, what stuck with me the most was how happy I was to help out. I don't think my friend agonized before picking up the phone and asking if his son could spend the afternoon with me. He knew that if I could do it I would, and if I couldn't I'd say so. No guilt, no long complicated story, no worry that he was asking too much. He had a need and I could help out.

Sometimes when I have a need I debate about asking for help. I wonder, *What will they think? Is it too much to ask? What if they can't do it?* These questions and others can delay me from picking up the phone or sending out an e-mail. What I need to remember in those moments is that I felt happy when asked, and grateful to be able to help. I felt included in that family's life, and others similarly will be happy to feel included in the life of my family. I'm not a juggler so I don't know this but, I think that it must be more complicated to juggle with other people than alone. But maybe it's not. Maybe with more hands it's easier to keep more balls in the air. It's definitely true for parenting—more willing and coordinated hands lighten the load, prevent dropping (losing, forgetting) the kids, and make everyone's lives easier.

Thank you, Lord, for friends who catch the ball when I am about to drop it, and who throw me the ball and let me be a part of their lives. Amen.

God Is My Co-Pilot

"'THEN WHO CAN BE saved?' Jesus looked at them and said, 'For mortals it is impossible, but not for God; with God all things are possible'" (Mark 10:26-27).

"God is my co-pilot." "Let go and let God." I thought about these bumper stickers recently as I contemplated the frenetic activity at my workplace. We are gearing up for the accreditation process, many students have been in need of assistance, the usual programs are running, and we are developing new programs. A lot has been done and there is a lot more to do. It can be tempting to do, do, do, running from one activity or meeting to another, and often that's what happens.

Then I read the story in Mark 10:17-27, about the rich man who is unwilling to sell all he owns and follow Jesus. I thought about what I am reluctant to let go of, and an answer came at once: I do not want to let go of control. I want to direct projects at work, and I like to be involved in many activities. To be honest, I want to do things my way, and often I want my kids and other people around me to do things my way! I like to plan ahead, be prepared, and not leave things to chance.

But what about leaving things to God? Where do I leave room for God to be at work in my life? God can't be my co-pilot if I don't let him onto the airplane! If I'm gripping the wheel tightly, determined to get to my destination all by myself, then God doesn't have a chance to influence my direction. Like the wealthy man who cannot follow Jesus without giving up his wealth, I cannot draw closer to God if I don't slow down long enough to let God get near to me.

Loving God, forgive my stubborn self-reliance that wears me out and shuts you out. Thank you for your Word that keeps me connected to you and to those I love. Amen.

Asking For Help

"WHEN YOU ASK FOR patience, God doesn't give you patience, he gives you opportunities to practice being patient" (God, in the movie *Evan Almighty*).

Asking for help is one area of my life where I could use some improvement, and recently God gave me an opportunity for practice. On vacation, I checked the voicemail on my cell phone and got a message from my boss asking me to e-mail her a one-page item a.s.a.p. I was annoyed that she called, and I did my share of complaining to a friend, but ultimately my boss's request really was time sensitive and I needed to send something to her.

It took me a while to get on the phone to my colleagues, and one after another my calls went unanswered. The fifth phone call yielded an answer, and in a short amount of time my staff member had e-mailed me the document I needed. I updated it which took about 30 minutes, then I e-mailed it to my boss. The time it took to accomplish the task was less than the amount of time I had spent stewing about it! And the real lesson for me was how easy it was for my colleague to help me, and how glad she was to help. My asking for help allowed me to get the job done with ease, and allowed her to be more involved in the work of our office. I didn't have to recreate the wheel on my own, just get a copy of it sent to me.

God, thank you for the helpers in my life who are there waiting to be asked. Remind me that asking for help is an invitation for involvement. Amen.

Being Present

Focus!

"MARTHA WAS DISTRACTED BY her many tasks; so she came to him and asked, 'Lord, do you not care that my sister has left me to do all the work by myself? Tell her then to help me.' But the Lord answered her, 'Martha, Martha, you are worried and distracted by many things; there is need of only one thing. Mary has chosen the better part, which will not be taken away from her'" (Luke 10:40-42).

It is Monday morning, I'm on my way to work, and I'm stuck in traffic. Not moving at all. It's been 20 minutes and I've driven about 100 yards. The traffic report on the radio says that both lanes of the bridge ahead of me are closed due to an accident. The frustrating thing is that I heard about the accident before I got to the traffic jam, while I still had a chance to change direction and take an alternate route. I listened to the radio, got into a different lane heading toward a different bridge, and then my mind wandered. I can't even say what I was thinking about – my weekend? work? the other news on the radio? (I was not on the phone!) Next thing I realized I had taken another turn and there I was heading for the first bridge and its traffic jam. Like being on autopilot, I was following my habitual pattern.

That realization, along with the time to reflect on it, made me think about how incredibly hard it can be to change our patterns, and how easily we get distracted from our course of action. I've noticed it in my work, where I turn to my e-mail to send a message to someone, then see another e-mail about a different subject and attend to it first because "it will only take a second," and the next thing I know I've responded to a half dozen e-mails and forgotten my original task. Or when I tell my kids that I'll play a game with them, then scurry around the house doing a few chores before we get started, because I'm distracted by my mental to-do list instead of focusing on spending time with my kids.

It is hard to focus on one thing and follow it to completion, especially in our world of multi-tasking, where it can seem inefficient to do only one thing at a time. Sure, maybe I can make lunches and talk to someone on the phone, but am I really focused on what that person is saying? What would happen if I really focused on one thing at a time? Would I get as much done, because each thing could be done more quickly if there were no interruptions? And what would happen if I were less activity-oriented (doing) and more in tune to relationships (being) - with others, with my writing, with God? I think I'll start by noticing more when I get distracted, and what I get distracted by. I suspect that what I get distracted by isn't as important as it seems, and I'll feel less harried and more centered.

Lord, writing these essays draws me closer to you. When I avoid writing because I allow myself to be distracted, please remind me of what matters most—being fully present to your presence in my life throughout each day. Amen.

My To-Do List

"I'D RATHER VISIT THE dusty home of a person with a dusted off Bible than the dust-free home of a person with a dusty Bible" (Unknown).

Call John. That was one of the items on my to-do list. Not that I would forget to call! I love him and we call each other almost every day. I put it on my to-do list last weekend so that I made time for it and honored it, and didn't fit it in after other tasks or chores.

Seeing it on my to-do list made me wonder about other important things that don't make it on the list, and whether I make enough time for them in my life or whether they get fit in around the chores. Things like going to church. I do it every Sunday that I'm home, but it isn't on my calendar. Or spending time during the week in meditation or prayer. That doesn't make the list, but maybe it should. It is as important in my life (probably more so!) than some of the other items: make pesto, send a thank-you note, text Leslie about the concert in the park, line up a dog walker for Luna for Monday. Certainly I won't forget to do the things I think are important and the things I value, but I put so many other things on the list that the unwritten ones get rushed, or I'm tired or distracted while doing them. In my busy life it's easy to do many things but none of them fully. Listening to my kids, listening for God, being present in my interactions with loved ones near and far—these are the things that bring joy, meaning, and energy to my life. I will put them at the top of my to-do list and give thanks for the opportunity to have them there.

What's on your to-do list this week? Make time for the things that you value!

Lord, thank you for moments of clarity when I see what matters. Amen.

Running In Front Of The Wave

"Now THERE WAS A great wind, so strong that it was splitting mountains and breaking rocks in pieces before the Lord, but the Lord was not in the wind; and after the wind an earthquake, but the Lord was not in the earthquake; and after the earthquake a fire, but the Lord was not in the fire; and after the fire a sound of sheer silence" (1 Kings 19:11-12).

You've probably done it, just like I do. Gone from activity to activity, chore to chore, task to task, generating items for my to-do list faster than I can check them off. Sometimes there is a flow of positive energy and an ease of motion. Other times there is an undercurrent of tension, a knot in my stomach, anxiety. By staying in motion I can distract myself from sadness, loneliness, upset, anger, grief, fear, and pain. But eventually the wave of emotion will catch up with me, maybe getting bigger the more I try to avoid it. Either way, sooner or later, it will come crashing over me.

Sometimes it comes unexpectedly, catching me off guard and adding to my feelings of emotional turbulence. Other times I recognize what I am doing and I allow myself to be still, letting the wave wash over me, honoring those emotions and letting myself feel them (knowing that I will be able to get on my feet afterwards, however shakily). Better to let the wave crest, crash, and then ebb away, leaving a clearing like when a storm blows past leaving blue skies and freshly washed leaves in its path. Then I can feel relief and peace, having cleared out the previous emotions. The rain of my tears softens the sadness and fears of my heart and opens it to happiness, laughter, joy, and the next experience in my life.

Lord, thank you for the moments when I can stop my running and hear your still small voice. Amen.

Just Doing It

"'Now go, and I will be with your mouth and teach you what you are to speak.' But [Moses] said, 'O my Lord, please send someone else'" (Exodus 4: 12-13).

I just planted crocuses. Yes, I bought crocus bulbs last fall, didn't plant them, put them in the basement, and now they are sprouting. So a few days ago I put dirt in two pretty pots, put in bulbs, and watered them. There wasn't enough room for all the bulbs so some stayed in the bag, sitting on my kitchen counter. Finally, today, realizing that my weekend is coming to a close and accepting the fact that conditions for planting won't be any better tomorrow (my conditions being time and energy), I stuck the last dozen bulbs in the ground. I used the dandelion spade to dig under the grass enough to push the bulb in the dirt and that was that. It's supposed to rain tonight so I didn't even water them.

Sometime in my future I hope to be able to garden at a more leisurely pace, spending time preparing the ground, mapping out placement of plants according to size and color and sun tolerance, and enjoying the planting. But for now my plants are lucky to make it into the dirt. Fortunately, that's really all they need! As I plant—even in speed-planting mode—I do take the time to marvel at the wonders of dirt and water and plants. Flower bulbs, vegetable seeds, all are amazingly self-sufficient, at least in getting started. Some need more tending than others as they grow and blossom or bear fruit, but really, once in the ground they just need some water and sunshine.

Planting those last bulbs took about 3 minutes, maybe less. I'd spent much more time than that just thinking about planting them! So too, in other areas of my life I spend more time thinking than doing. E-mailing those photos? Sorting the paperwork for taxes? Sewing the button on the jacket? Those are small things, but my procrastination happens around big things too, like calling the handyman to get my porch fixed (I've been talking about it for over a year), or starting the chapter that's due in June. Fortunately, as in my gardening, I've found that getting started is the hard part. It doesn't have to be perfect at the start, and it may never make it to whatever "perfect" picture I have in my mind, but getting started sure beats not getting started. For some of the projects on my "to-do" list, getting started means making a phone call—that's it!

The Nike motto of "just do it" captures the spirit of this first day of spring. The bulbs are going to sprout whether I put them in the ground or not. They practically yell "Just plant us! Don't worry about finding the best place or the best time!" Similarly, my blog yells "Just write! Get started!" What things in your life are urging you to just do them? Go sow those seeds, and don't be afraid to get dirty!

Lord, thank you for the miracles of bulbs, seeds, and spring. Help me to take action even when I think I'm not ready, and especially when I think too much. Amen.

Being Playful

Luna And The Loons

"Yonder is the sea, great and wide, creeping things innumerable are there, living things both small and great. There go the ships, and Leviathan, that you formed to sport in it" (Psalm 104:25-26).

Luna, our dog, loves to fish. She's laying on the grass next me now, but only because she's been in the water for the past five hours and she's exhausted. Luna fishes by wading in the water along the shoals off the shoreline, sometimes getting deep enough to swim (this is not too deep as her legs are disproportionately short for her body). She follows sunfish and tiny bass, and she bites at bubbles and growls at the fish. All the while her tail wags high in the air, in case you couldn't tell that she's having the time of her life. Yesterday she added to her fishing technique by sticking her entire head—up to her collar—under the water! Her hind end was out of the water, tail wagging, and her head moved back and forth following the path of the minnow. She kept her head under water for six seconds one time, and ten seconds another time. We didn't know it when we named her, but apparently Luna is part loon. She's black and sleek, her feet are webbed (and we thought that was some Lab in her hybrid mix), and she dives for fish.

Luna is very dedicated to this new mission in her life. Earlier today we went for a boat ride while she was in the water and she barely glanced our way. We debated putting her in the house while we were gone, but we would have had to haul her out of the water, put her in her crate sopping wet, and then she would have howled after we drove off. So we left her in the water and she was still there when we returned. Never mind that she hasn't caught a fish yet, and probably never will. She is enthusiastic, passionate, and in her glory, and we are getting a lot of pleasure watching her.

This is a good lesson for me, as I'm prone to being practical. Luna's lesson for me is to enjoy the journey and not worry so much if I'm not sure of the destination. To frolic and play and get lost in doing something that I love, whether I will ever gain mastery of it or not, or whether it has a practical purpose or not. To delight in God's creation—the lake, the fish, Luna, the loons, my kids and their neighbor friend jumping in the water themselves, the sun and breeze on my back as I write. To sleep, exhausted, after a day of reveling in nature and its gifts.

Lord, how wonderful is your creation and your creatures! Thank you for the privilege of living among them. Amen.

Playing Pinochle

"AND [HE] SAID: 'TRULY I tell you, unless you change and become like children, you will never enter the kingdom of heaven'" (Matthew 18:3).

I don't know how to play pinochle, or at least I didn't up until last summer. That's when my kids learned how to play. They taught me and we spent some wonderful time together playing cards. It was one morning during our vacation that the kids decided to learn to play pinochle. They set off in search of instructions, first looking in a book, then turning to the internet. They found printed and audio instructions, and they rapidly learned the game. I imagine that what went through their minds during this process was pretty straight-forward: "I'd like to learn something new, I'll find out how, and I'll do it."

What went through my mind was this: *I've never played pinochle, I don't know anyone who does, it seems like a game that old people used to play, and I'll never learn to play it.* Yikes! As quickly as that I had decided that I was too old, *and that I was okay with that.* I got a glimpse of one way of being middle-aged—thinking that I've learned all I'm going to learn, and worse, not being upset about it! When I realized how my thoughts were going I could see the craziness of my complacence. But I almost didn't see it, almost buying into the thought that young people will learn new things and that older people will not. I almost lost the chance to learn something new, have fun with my kids, and give them the satisfaction of teaching me something they'd learned.

What new learning experience will be next for me? I don't know. But I do know that I have to be vigilant in keeping at bay thoughts of "been there, done that; haven't been there, not doing that." I have a lot to learn from the young people around me, and best of all, it can be a lot of fun!

Thank you, God, for the times when I pause and reflect in my everyday life. Keep me from complacent thoughts and actions. Keep my heart and mind open to new things. Amen.

Not Too Old For Songfest!

"The Lord said to Abraham, 'Why did Sarah laugh, and say, 'Shall I indeed bear a child, now that I am old?' Is anything too wonderful for the Lord?'" (Genesis 18: 13-14).

Last year I danced with four of my co-workers in Songfest, the annual dance competition at our college. We had a blast, and the students cheered us on enthusiastically. I've gotten a lot of positive comments about it since then. Songfest is a long-standing tradition where in prior decades student groups, choruses, and glee clubs sang. It has changed over the years to the point where groups do a dance routine to recorded music. We have a lot of talented students, so the choreography and dancing are impressive, and costumes, backdrops, and props round out the routines. It is a fun evening where our students strut their stuff and really get to shine.

Back in January when a couple of coworkers suggested that we form a group to dance, a large group of us laughed a lot and agreed to do it. Fast forward to mid-March when we actually started rehearsing, and I wondered if this was such a good idea. The enthusiasm of a dozen people had dwindled to five, and I was the oldest one by far. I wondered: *Would I look stupid? Was I too old to be doing this? What would the students think? What would my colleagues think?* Part of me hoped that the others would suggest that we not do it—it had been a fun idea, we had gotten some laughs out of it, but let's quit while we're ahead. They didn't make that suggestion and I kept my mouth shut, not wanting to be the one to bail out at the last minute. Both Victoria and Curtis had put a lot of time and energy into the choreography of our dance, and I wanted to support them.

In the days leading up to Songfest I got my priorities in order, remembering that I wanted to support and encourage my colleagues, show the students that we administrators could have fun too, and that, most of all, this wasn't about me! "Being too old" is a mindset, one not worthy of a child of God. Maybe that's why the phrase is "a *child* of God," so that as we age we stay connected to the joyful part of our souls, the parts that don't worry about grown up stuff like cleaning the house, paying the bills, or how we look to others. The focus of "being too old" is on ourselves, while "being a child of God" places the focus on our relationship to God. I'm sure God took delight in the energy, spirit and goodwill that was generated prior to and during Songfest. I know I did!

Lord, may I never be too old to dance, and to take delight in the company of your other children, young and old. Amen.

Being Positive

One Turn At A Time

"Therefore encourage one another and build up each other, as indeed you are doing" (1 Thessalonians 5:11).

"Just take one turn at a time!" I called to my son, Conor, as he made his way down the mountain on his snowboard. It was his fourth day on a snowboard, and the first that season. He had spent the morning on the ski-school slope, and now we had taken the chairlift to the top of the mountain. The green dotted trail on the map indicated that it was designed for beginners, but this was his first run on this kind of trail.

I skied and he snowboarded for 30 feet, and we'd stop. Then we would go 40 feet, stop, let some more experienced people pass us, and then we'd go again. At a steeper part of the trail he fell, then fell again, and yet again, finding it hard to get to his feet on the steeper and narrower slope. He tumbled some more and got snow up the back of his jacket. He was working hard, but he never said he couldn't do it, he just kept getting up and trying some more. Gradually, one turn at a time, he went further and further between falls, until he was able to take some turns and then stop without falling. We both cheered as he experienced the exhilaration of accomplishment, and I experienced the thrill of seeing his dramatic growth in skill and confidence.

Taking one turn at a time is a great way to approach our lives too. Taking one turn at a time, one task at a time, one day at a time, no matter what daunting thing is facing us. It's good to have someone encouraging us along the way, reminding us not to look too far down the mountain to all the turns ahead. For me it's fitness. I tell myself that it's not worth doing if I don't have an hour to walk or bike, but then I don't do it at all. Sometimes it's a project at work that I avoid (the 10-page report with various appendices), telling myself that it will take many hours to accomplish, yet not blocking out the time and not getting started even with one hour.

What is it that you are avoiding? Maybe you want to lose weight, or stop smoking, or are facing a difficult course of study. Maybe you have lost your job and are overwhelmed by the process of starting a search. Achieving the goals we have for our futures, big or small, begins with a single step—a phone call, an e-mail, a walk around the block—and telling other people about it so that they can encourage us to take the next step, and the next. It won't be long before we'll be able to look back up the mountain and admire the progress we've made along the trail we're on.

God of encouragement, thank you for those around us who call us to be our best, one turn at a time. Amen.

The Pot Luck Dinner

"AND DO NOT KEEP striving for what you are to eat and what you are to drink, and do not keep worrying. For it is the nations of the world that strive after all these things, and your Father knows that you need them. Instead, strive for his kingdom, and these things will be given to you as well" (Luke 12:29-31).

On Sunday I attended a pot-luck dinner at church to celebrate Epiphany. We brought food that represented our ethnic heritage, so the meal was a wonderful variety of delicious recipes. I enjoyed a main course with food from Greece, Jamaica, Nigeria, and the southern U.S. I didn't pause long before eating three different desserts, and then felt uncomfortably stuffed! On the way home I mentally kicked myself for not fully appreciating the main course foods before jumping to the sweets.

Then it occurred to me that is was very much like living life in "ordinary" time in the church calendar, which comes after celebrating the holidays (holy days) of Advent, Christmas, and Epiphany. Ordinary time is filled with weeks of work and weekends of activities, events and time spent with friends. The good events and moments of my weekdays and weekends are the substance of my life. The people at work and evening meetings at church provide me with much of my social contacts and enjoyment; the time spent with my sons after work and school is precious. These people and times are the meat and potatoes, the bread and pasta, the fruits and vegetables of my life.

Holidays are filled with special treats, from food to events to travel. They are like the icing and the cake, commemorating extraordinary occasions. My feeling stuffed from the richness of too many desserts was a good reminder to savor and affirm the nutritional building blocks, as it were, of my life. This week I will take the time to appreciate and give thanks for the joy and fulfillment to be had in the ordinary weeks of my life. I will recognize and celebrate the extraordinary gift that the ordinary is! How blessed I am to have people who I can count on, and to be a part of a faith community that comes together in good times and bad, in everyday and holiday.

Lord, thank you for providing a steady diet of love and reassurance, no matter the time of year. Amen.

Detour Ahead

"AND HAVING BEEN WARNED in a dream not to return to Herod, they left for their own country by another road" (Matthew 2:12).

I love to drive. Whether I am watching farmland, hills, lakes and rivers roll by, or driving through small towns, looking at houses, shops, schools, monuments, I find it relaxing and a good opportunity to reflect. I get frustrated, however, driving on poorly marked roads, where signs are missing or turned. Especially annoying are detours where the first turn is marked and then there are no more signs! Locals may know the side roads but out-of-towners do not. Sometimes I have to stop driving, study a map, or ask someone else for directions.

The parallels to my life are remarkable. I am happy living my days on a well-marked path, where the twists and turns and views are predictable. I can plan for birthdays and holidays (spectacular view out the right side window!), and practice preventative health care by getting enough sleep, eating well, and taking vitamins (take the car for an oil change regularly). Of course, like roads, my life sometimes is under construction and that involves detours. What's next for me at work? Is it time for a career change? What about a new relationship? I can try out new "side roads," but unlike driving, my destination may not be all that clear. There are many roads to happiness, fulfillment, and contributing to others, not just one superhighway. And, unlike most of my driving, life is not just about the destination. Happiness, fulfillment, and contributing to others are part of the drive itself, to be savored, and like some small towns they can be missed if I'm driving too fast, too eager to get to my future.

When driving, I can get a better sense of where I'm going if I stop to read a map. Maybe a cross-road will be marked, and although it won't be the road for me it will help guide me. Studying Scripture can be the road map for my life, giving guidance when I face a crossroad or a detour. Although it does not give turn-by-turn directions, the Bible gives me some rules of the road and practical advice for any situation. The Bible is full of wonderful examples of people who have gone before me without a detailed map, trusting in their dreams, listening for the words of prophets, angels, and Jesus to guide them on their journey.

Finally, when I'm lost, both in the car and in my life, I can turn to others for assistance. Sometimes my family, friends, co-workers, and church community will have some answers, and sometimes they will not, but their company is a reminder that there is no one "right" path, and reassurance that whatever road I take I will not be alone.

Lord, thank you for the directional signs in my life, and for the spectacular views along the journey. Amen.

Salt

"You are the salt of the earth; but if salt has lost its taste, how can its saltiness be restored? It is no longer good for anything, but is thrown out and trampled under foot" (Matthew 5:13).

Obviously, the Israelites were not living with the severe kind of winter we've been having this year! Their use of salt was related to food and their bodies—seasoning food, preserving food, and essential to the chemical balance of their bodies. Salt without its salty taste was no good. How refreshing for us, then, that even something that might be declared no good in the kitchen (especially for people with high blood pressure and other conditions) can be an important element in getting around safely amidst the snow and ice. Salt is not the only thing that can give us traction on the sidewalks and roads in the winter, and its overuse is deteriorating the cement and metal structures of our roads and bridges, but today, in light of the Scripture above, I am choosing to see it as another example of how things that we declare useless can be redeemed.

"You are the salt of the earth." In saying this, Jesus tells us that we have an important role to play in bringing God's kingdom to earth. Nice to know, though, that we all don't have the same role to play. Seasoning, preserving, nutritional balance, traction and melting—which way will you be the salt of the earth? Think your usefulness is over? Think you or your ideas are no good? Not to worry! God's vision for us is not limited by our lack of imagination, or our limitations of place and time. If you've got an idea for furthering God's kingdom, I encourage you to pray, be bold, and give it a try. It might be just what's needed to complete the feast.

Lord, we say that variety is the spice of life. Help us to bring out our own variety of saltiness in our lives, so that we may be of service to others, and glorify you. Amen.

Sunrise Reflection

"THE HEAVENS ARE TELLING the glory of God; and the firmament proclaims his handiwork" (Psalm19:1).

I've been getting up at sunrise (not a difficult thing to do in December), taking a few moments to watch the beautiful display of sun and clouds. Red, purple, pink, and orange—the colors and patterns are a stunning expression of God's glory as the day begins.

Today the sunrise was a pale peach colored glow. *Not really much*, I thought. Then I realized that it heralds a new day, with the same opportunities as any other day. It is no less glorious of a day just because the sunrise wasn't spectacular. *Just like me*, I thought! I don't start out spectacularly every day (probably not most days) but nevertheless each day has the same potential to be amazing. And each day I have the potential to be amazing. I'm reminded not to judge a person by her appearance, and not to judge a day by its sunrise. Maybe I'll shine a little brighter today and give the sun a break!

Dear Lord, thank you for this day and all the potential it holds. Amen.

You Are Not Alone

The Tow Pound

"THE LIGHT SHINES IN the darkness, and the darkness did not overcome it" (John 1:5).

When I wrote "Stop Lights," I had no idea that two days later I would have a road block much bigger to deal with than traffic lights. It happened in Manhattan, where my friend Leslie and I were meeting for dinner and then attending a party with a "Roaring 20's" theme. I parked my car on the street, pretty sure that the open spot was in fact a valid parking place. I paid the nearby meter, put the receipt on the dashboard, dismissed the voice of doubt about whether the "No Parking" sign ahead stretched all the way back to my car, and went on my way.

Lo and behold, when we came back to the place where I had parked my car, the car was gone. Fighting the urge to cry, and ignoring the voices in my head that were saying *I told you so! That spot was too good to be true!* I instead listened to Leslie, who knew what to do since she had been in this situation once before.

We walked to the corner and down another block to an ATM, remarking that at least it was a beautiful night out—warm, breezy, and dry. I got cash and then we hailed a nearby cab (another blessing), and we went to the NYPD Tow Pound. The Tow Pound is a warehouse, basically, full of towed cars, with a trailer attached where you go to pay the money required to spring your car out of the warehouse. In we walked, in our black cocktail dresses, high heels, and black feather boas (it was a Roaring 20's party, remember?)

What greeted us was a long line of people waiting to be helped, none of them happy. A man stormed past us and out the door, snarling with a southern twang, "I'm never coming back to this *%##@ city again!" I could sympathize. Leslie sat down among the other people waiting. I stood in line, praying for peace and calm. Eventually I reached the counter, gave the worker my driver's license, and was told to wait. By that time Leslie had started talking to a family, and we shared our stories of how it was that we were ending our evenings with this experience. They complimented us on our outfits, we laughed, and Leslie reminded me of the way that I had seemingly tempted fate by writing on my blog about being stopped at traffic lights. We laughed a lot at the lighted deli-counter-style sign that read "Now serving 00"—it never changed!—and we were disappointed that no picture-taking was permitted. The warmth of our conversation dispelled the dreariness of the room.

The presence of my friend and of these newly-made friends was such a gift. I silently thanked God for the resources that I had, the people who were making it an experience to remember with a smile and a laugh rather than tears, and the ability to choose my attitude about it all. Stuck at the Tow Pound? Absolutely! Stuck in life? Not at all, thanks to a solid grounding of faith in finding the silver lining in a bad situation.

Finally, our names were called, we paid our fees, and said goodbye to our new friends. All told, it took about two hours to get my car and start the drive home (which took very little time because at that hour there was very little traffic!) Another opportunity to laugh about the incident came the next morning when I looked at the receipt I had been given when I paid for my car. Stamped across it in big black capital letters was one word: REDEEMED.

Thank you, God, for your redeeming grace that assures us that your light <u>always</u> will overcome darkness. Amen.

Love Is Like A Life Raft

"WITH LOVE, HAPPINESS IS multiplied and sorrow divided" (Unknown).

The privilege of having love includes the certainty of pain. Good thing that loving relationships fill us with so much joy and laughter, because the pain we feel when those relationships end can be so intense that we sometimes wonder how we can go on with our lives.

This essay is for my friend Susan, whose dear friend Susie died. Vibrant, loving, generous, Susie lived her life with a positive outlook and a spirit of abundance. She left behind family and friends filled with grief. Susan told me that at the funeral they comforted each other with stories of Susie's life, knowing what a gift it was to each of them. As the weeks, months, and years go by I am sure that Susan still will talk to Susie, knowing that Susie's spirit will be nearby, eager to hear the news of the neighborhood and still available for comfort as well as cheer.

There is tremendous comfort to be had when we share our grief with others. It can be painful to remember the person who died, or the marriage that ended, but I've found that when I carry my grief around inside me it wears me out, eats me up, and festers, biding its time until my defenses are weakened and it rushes out in unexpected and unpleasant ways. I've learned that it is better to let the tears come sooner rather than later, and better yet to be with a loved one—family or friend—who can hand me a tissue, hold me close, and hang on, riding out the storm of emotion with me. After the tears there is always relief and release—relief from the tension and release from the pain of grief. Love is like a life raft that buoys us up through the storms that are sure to come in our lives.

God, thank you for my friendship with Susan, and for the many other people with whom I share love. I am reminded that love is a blessing to be treasured, nurtured, and extended to others when they are caught in their own storms of grief. Amen.

Reeling In The Big Fish

"AND JESUS SAID TO them, 'Follow me and I will make you fish for people'" (Mark 1:17).

Recently my friend Marie told me about a mistake she made at work. She works for a not-for-profit organization, and has been there for a couple of years, steadily meeting and cultivating donors. Through the internet she had become acquainted with a potential donor who had indicated that he was well connected and that he had the ability to make a very large gift. He was related tangentially to the organization but he claimed an affinity for it, so she did a bit of online research about him and then set up a meeting over lunch. She was tremendously excited about the possibility of landing a really big donor.

When I talked to her after the meeting she was disappointed and embarrassed. The potential donor had fabricated most of what he told her previously, and probably was doing his own bit of fishing—after all, he did get a nice lunch. She learned a lesson in trust—be willing to believe things that people tell you, but look for verification and be thorough as you carry out your background research. It was also a lesson in pride. As she told me, "I was hoping to reel in a very big fish, but all I got was a bunch of weeds!" Her desire to make a big splash at the office had dulled her sense of caution. While she thought she was the one doing the fishing, she ended up being the one to take the bait. Fortunately, all she lost was a small amount of time and money, and a bit of pride. In turn she gained a portion of humility with a side order of healthy skepticism.

She washed it down with the compassionate laughter of trusted friends, and called it a day.

Lord, without you we fish in vain. Remind us that with you as our guide, our catch will be bountiful. Amen.

Missing You

"I WILL NOT LEAVE you orphaned; I am coming to you" (John 14:18).

I spent most of the day alone. I called my parents and some friends, but didn't reach them. I didn't call others who I knew were unavailable. I played with Luna, and I did some reading, then I did errands and had a good time working in the yard. It was a beautiful day, an ideal spring day in my opinion—low humidity, blue sky, trees in full pink bloom, grass bright green and growing like crazy. I stayed busy—always easy to do—but I know that staying busy sometimes is my way of avoiding other things. Like how much I miss my kids, friends, and family. I've moved around, I've gotten divorced, I live far from my parents. I've made choices that have allowed for wonderful new relationships and new friends, but sometimes, like now when I've had plenty of "alone time," I miss them and it hurts a lot. Fortunately, I know that I will see my kids soon, and I will see friends and family soon too. I am thankful for the time that we have together. I may be sad when we are apart, but I am so grateful for their presence in my life, and I look forward to the next time we can be together.

The parallel to Easter is striking. On Good Friday Christians remember the mourning, pain, and loss that Christ's followers were experiencing as he was crucified. Three long days later, his disciples were astonished and overjoyed to see Christ risen from the dead. While Christ had been alive with them they were not fully aware of what precious time it was. Their separation made his reappearance all the more joyous, the reunion more special. And, as he had told them, they would not be alone. Although the Holy Spirit was not a physical presence, the disciples were connected with Christ through it. In our connection to Christ through the Holy Spirit we are not alone. In my times of pain, loneliness, fear, and uncertainty, I know that I am loved by the One who is the source of all love.

Lord, thank you for your presence and comfort in my times of sorrow. Amen.

Fear Not

"IN THAT REGION THERE were shepherds living in the fields, keeping watch over their flock by night. Then an angel of the Lord stood before them, and the glory of the Lord shone around them, and they were terrified. But the angel said to them 'Do not be afraid; for see—I am bringing you good news of great joy for all the people'" (Luke 2:8-10).

It is fitting that I am choosing to write about fear, as writing is what I am most fearful of these days. I made a commitment to myself and shared it with a friend: I would write one reflective essay per week. One per week seemed very doable, until the days passed and now here it is, the due date I assigned myself. One thing I'm learning is that I'm not afraid of writing, exactly. It's more that I'm afraid of writing badly, or of having nothing to write. It's so much easier to *say* that I'll write something than actually to *do* it! This holds true in many areas of life: "I'll (fill in the blank) tomorrow"— clean the house, start exercising, stop smoking, break off the relationship, restore the relationship, tackle that project at work, go back to school. You name the activity, it's much less threatening to think about it than to do it.

Another thing I'm realizing is that avoidance of fear is a very powerful, though not purposeful, motivator. I've accomplished a lot today before finally sitting down to write, all important things on my "to do" list. With the end-of-the-year deadline approaching I've filled out my health care reimbursement form. To do that I organized my files, filing about eight months of bills and receipts so that I could find the documents necessary to submit the form. Then I went out and bought a printer/copier/scanner so I could copy the forms and receipts before mailing them. I'd been meaning to buy that kind of machine for at least a year. So much accomplished! I even exercised today, which always is on my "to do" list but rarely gets done. Today my avoidance of the fear of writing has paid off in productive ways. But the problem with the avoidance of fear as a motivator is that later, after all the other activity is accomplished, the desired/feared activity still is not done and the fear is undiminished.

As I reflect on my day so far, I can see how my anxiety creeps in, like a little critter, and I fool myself into thinking that if I just stay busy it won't land on me. Like if I jump around flapping my hands when a bee buzzes too close, I think I am avoiding harm. But in my frantic activity I'm just antagonizing the bee and wearing myself out. The anxiety still is there waiting to land, but I can avoid it by staying busy and then saying that it's too late, or I'm too tired to write.

So why did I stop flailing around and start to write today? Not just because I said I would, but because I told my friend I would, and I don't want to admit that I haven't done any writing. And ultimately I'm tired of *pretending* I want to write. I don't want to hear myself making hollow claims any more. Avoiding fear is a lot of work, both physically and emotionally, so why not sit down and write? Other people write reflections on life and publish them. Why not me? My doubting self might think *my writing is not good enough*, or worse, *I'm not good enough*, but the part of my self that believes in God-given gifts knows that I like to write, and that in following such a path I won't be led astray.

Believing that "nothing is impossible with God" is a powerful and purposeful motivator, as it makes clear that I'm not in this activity alone. I will trust that once I start on this path the next steps will become available to me, and then I will face whatever fears may be waiting around the bend, again trusting in God's promised presence.

Loving and powerful God, thank you for your constant presence and love which dispels all fear. Amen.

I Want Answers

"The Lord is my shepherd, I shall not be in want. He makes me lie down in green pastures, he leads me beside still waters; he restores my soul. He leads me in right paths for his name's sake" (Psalm 23: 1-3).

At work I found myself feeling very anxious, and realized that I wasn't producing what I thought my boss wanted. My report was coming up with more questions than answers. My boss reassured me that good questions are valuable outcomes, leading to more productive research and perhaps more informed answers. My anxiety eased, but a doubting voice inside my head still wanted answers. It can be difficult to live in the pre-conclusion space, content to be on a journey of inquiry, accompanied by the unknown.

This week my goal was to do some journaling about my future, seeking a sense of what I'm being drawn to do. There were opportunities to write, but I avoided them, choosing to fill my time with errands and housework. Until this morning when I had an unexpected hour of available time, and I observed myself rushing to fill it with things that didn't need to be done yet, like preparing dinner or drilling holes in the closet for hooks. Finally I stopped those thoughts and asked myself what I was running away from by avoiding journaling. I realized that I don't have answers to my questions about the future, and that made me anxious. If I avoid the questions, I avoid an immediate sense of discomfort, and I can reassure myself that I will write in my journal when I am better prepared. That is, when I have a better sense of what I want to do with my future.

You can see how this is a perfect circle of avoidance! I don't want to write until I have a clearer view of my future (goals, ambitions, desires), but I won't have a clearer view until I write about my thoughts and ideas. It seems that I want answers, but I'm not willing to face the uncomfortable process of asking questions. More accurately, I don't like the uncertainty of not knowing what the answer is (as if there is only one right answer for my future). It is likely that there are many answers, some better than others, but no single answer being the right one.

I find reassurance in Scripture which reminds me that, contrary to being accompanied by the unknown in this process of inquiry, God is always with me on my journey. Indeed, I believe that is what God desires—for us to draw close to God in our journeying, and as a result of our journeying. By journaling, I can document my thoughts and actions along my journey, but more than that, writing allows me to explore my ideas and be present to my experience of life. Writing enables me to pause and think about who I am being and becoming, rather than getting caught up in what I've done or am doing. When I write, I am drawn near to God. I can be comfortable in asking questions for which I don't yet have the answers, confident that I am not traveling alone.

Lord, enable me to stay near you on my journey, and to be present to your guidance. Amen.

CPSIA information can be obtained at www.ICGtesting.com
Printed in the USA
BVOW022211120712

295048BV00001B/1/P